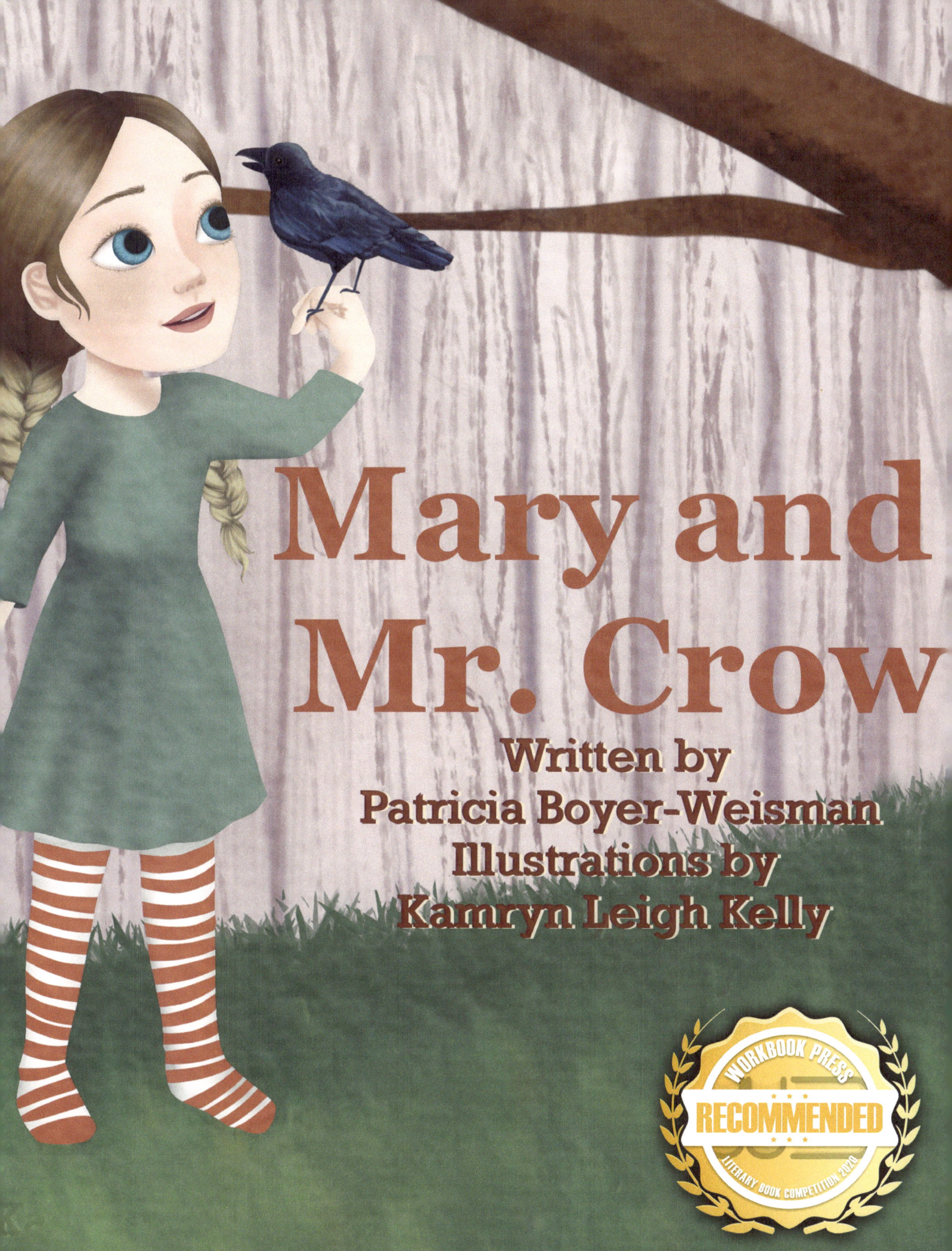

Mary and Mr. Crow

Solve a Problem

By Patricia Boyer-Weisman

"Mr. and Mrs. Sparrow why are you making so much noise?" asked Mary, who was ten years old.

"Mr. Crow, why are you calling and so angry? Old Grandma Finch, why aren't you sitting on the fence like you always do? None of you are sitting and eating on the bird feeders."

Mr. and Mrs. Sparrow shouted, "He's a thief!"

"He's more than a thief. He should be run out of town!" cawed Mr. Crow.

Old Grandma Finch said, "I'm too old to fight for my place at the feeder."

"Tell me why you all are saying this?" asked Mary.

Mr. Crow said, "What's going on is that he steals our food."

"It's shameful," added Old Grandma Finch.

"I fill the feeders every day," said Mary.

"Yes," said Mr. Crow, "but he steals our food before we can eat it. He barges in, takes over the feeders, and leaves quickly."

"He doesn't ask. He just takes," said Old Grandma Finch.

"Who?" asked Mary.

"The squirrel," answered Mrs. Sparrow.

"He's a stinking rodent," said Mr. Crow.

"He's rude and has no manners," said Old Grandma Finch.

Mary said, "Tomorrow when I fill the feeders I will wait for him."

Suddenly Mr. Squirrel arrived and jumped on a feeder.

Mary approached Mr. Squirrel. "Why are you stealing food when clearly it is not meant for you. You are upsetting the birds by stealing from their feeder."

"I am hungry and I have a family to feed," Mr. Squirrel replied. "My children cry for food."

"But this food is for the birds," said Mary, "not you."

"That's the problem," said Mr. Squirrel. "What about me? You feed Mr. and Mrs. Sparrow, Mr. Crow, and Old Grandma Finch, but there's no food for me."

Mary said, "If we can find food for you, will you no longer steal from the bird feeder? Maybe if you ask politely and then wait, the others will be kind enough to share."

"That has not worked in the past," said Mr. Squirrel. "They see me as an outsider. I do not have feathers, but I am hungry just like they are. They think I am a thief before I have a chance to talk. They judge me as crude and having no manners, just because I have fur and no feathers, so I take what I want."

"I am going to ask them to meet with you so that you can explain your story," said Mary. "Will you come and tell them about your family?"

"I can but it will do no good," said Mr. Squirrel. "They only see me as different, but I have the same needs as they do. They hate me."

"No," said Mary. "They hate that you take their food without asking. Have some faith and meet with them. Tell your story. Maybe you can even become friends."

"Friends? They scold me and fly at me to knock me off a branch. They spread tales about me."

"I understand," said Mary. "But will you come to a meeting and talk to them?"

"If you will be there," answered Mr. Squirrel.

"I'll be there," Mary said.

"Mr. Crow will you meet with Mr. Squirrel and ask the others to come?" asked Mary. "I know you can convince them to come. Mr. Squirrel is no different than each of you. He has a story similar to all of you."

"I will ask all of them," said Mr. Crow, "but I have to convince them that the meeting will turn out well."

When Mr. Crow asked his friends to attend the meeting, the Sparrows said," He's a common thief. He is not one of us. Where are his feathers?"

"We do not like his stealing," added Old Grandma Finch, "but maybe it won't do any harm to listen to his story."

"All right, have him come tomorrow at feeding time," said Mr. and Mrs. Sparrow. "Let's hope he does not plan to sneak in and just take the food like always."

Old Grandma Finch said, "now let's given him a chance. The little girl will be there so I am willing to listen."

"Thank you my friends," said Mary. "I will tell him to be here at 8:00 in the morning when I fill the feeders."

"All right, and he better be on time. None of his sneaking around," said the Sparrows.

Old Grandma Finch said again, "Now, now let's hear him out. Let's let him explain."

"Thank you, my friends, for trusting me," said Mary. "I will tell him to be here at 8:00 in the morning when I fill the feeders."

Mr. Crow said, "Tell him not to be late. No sneakiness or I'll peck him hard."

Mary told Mr. Squirrel she had talked to Mr. and Mrs. Sparrow, Mr. Crow, and Old Grandma Finch. They agreed to meet with him at the morning feeding and he should not be late.

"Will you come and not be late?" Mary asked Mr. Squirrel.

"Yes, but I know they do not like me."

Mary said, "They do not know you! Come and let them know you and why you take their food."

"Yes, I'll come."

Mr. and Mrs. Sparrow, Mr. Crow, and Old Grandma Finch waited the next morning in the tree where the feeders hung.

Mary brought food to put in the feeders.

"Well, where is he? He's late!" said the birds.

"Only five minutes, I sure he'll explain," said Mary.

Mr. Squirrel showed up in a panic. "I am sorry to be late. I had to find someone to watch my little ones. This morning my old mother was not feeling well and my brother did not come home last night. I had no choice but to leave them sleeping in their bed so I must make this quick. I am afraid Mr. Owl will wake up and he likes small baby squirrels for lunch."

Mr. and Mrs. Sparrow ask, "Where is your wife?"

"Isn't she watching your little ones?" asked Mr. Crow. "That is her job."

Old Grandma Finch said, "Friends, listen now quickly he talks. See how he moves around . Let's give him a chance to explain."

"My wife died when my babies were born. She was just too weak," said Mr. Squirrel. "We never have enough food to eat. Because of all the people building new homes, there are fewer trees, fewer nuts, and many squirrels find it harder to locate food."

"So you steal?" asked Mr. Crow.

Old Grandma Finch said, "Mr. Crow, listen please."

Mr. Squirrel answered, "Yes, I guess I do. I have not thought it was stealing. You have so much food. Every day the little girl fills your feeders.

My babies are hungry. My grandmother is hungry. My brother, when he shows up, is hungry. I am the only one trying to find enough food for my family. I have to move fast each time I go out to find food. I have to get back before Mr. Owl wakes up."

Old Grandma Finch said, "Friends we have plenty. Shame on us for not asking Mr. Squirrel what his story is. I think we should apologize and invite him to supper."

Mr. Crow caws, "I apologize for calling you a thief."

Mary said, "I think everyone should apologize and forgive. Now we know his story and I believe him. Each of us have similar stories that we could share. Let's not judge one another."

"Sparrows weren't you looking for food when I hung up the bird feeder?" asked Mary. "Mr. Crow, did you not sit on my fence and watch for the seeds that fell to the ground? And Old Grandma Finch, when you had trouble sitting on one feeder with the others, didn't I put up another feeder?"

"Yes," answered Mr. Crow.

Old Grandma Finch said, "You're right. I am ashamed."

"No need to be ashamed. Just ask why our friend eats your food and why he such a hurry," said Mary. "And Mr. Squirrel, ask for help. Tell your story. These friends have good hearts and can understand your many responsibilities."

Mr. and Mrs. Sparrow, Mr. Crow, and Old Grandma Finch all said together, "Mr. Squirrel, please join us at the feeders."

Mr. Crow said, "I can help watch your babies when you need to gather food."

Mr. and Mrs. Sparrow said, "We can help find your brother when he does not show up."

Old Grandma Finch said, "I need someone to talk to sometime so I can visit with your grandmother."

And Mary said, "I will hang another feeder and put nuts and corn in it. I will be there at 8:00 in the morning and 6:00 in the evening to fill all the feeders. There will be plenty of seeds, corn, and nuts for all of you to eat. You are all my friends and I am glad to have a new one. Maybe we will even welcome a few more friends, and we will not be so quick to judge."

Mary, Mr. and Mrs. Sparrow, Mr. Crow, and Old Grandma Finch said to Mr. Squirrel, "you are welcome here as part of our family."

THE END

Copyright @2022 by (Patricia Boyer Weismen)

All rights reserved. No part of this book may be reproduced in any form or by any electronic or mechanical means, including information storage and retrieval systems, without permission in writing from the publisher, except by reviewers, who may quote brief passages in a review.

This publication contains the opinions and ideas of its author. It is intended to provide helpful and informative material on the subjects addressed in the publication. The author and publisher specifically disclaim all responsibility for any liability, loss or risk, personal or otherwise, which is incurred as a consequence, directly or indirectly, of the use and application of any of the contents of this book.

WORKBOOK PRESS LLC
187 E Warm Springs Rd,
Suite B285, Las Vegas, NV 89119, USA

Website: https://workbookpress.com/
Hotline: 1-888-818-4856
Email: admin@workbookpress.com

Ordering Information:
Quantity sales. Special discounts are available on quantity purchases by corporations, associations, and others. For details, contact the publisher at the address above.

Library of Congress Control Number:
ISBN-13: 978-1-957618-14-2 (Paperback Version)
978-1-957618-15-9 (Digital Version)

REV. DATE: 01/26/22

www.ingramcontent.com/pod-product-compliance
Lightning Source LLC
Chambersburg PA
CBHW041100070526
44579CB00002B/25